ELEPHANTS AND Golden Thrones

❧ INSIDE CHINA'S FORBIDDEN CITY ❧

ELEPHANTS AND Golden Thrones

✦INSIDE CHINA'S FORBIDDEN CITY✦

WRITTEN BY

TRISH MARX

PHOTOGRAPHS AND PHOTOGRAPH SELECTION BY

ELLEN B. SENISI

Foreword by Li Ji, Executive Deputy Director, The Palace Museum

ABRAMS BOOKS FOR YOUNG READERS ✦ NEW YORK

Foreword

A young man is roused from his slumber by a crowd of attendants, then rushed to take his place on the imperial throne. This young man is none other than Kangxi, a great emperor of the Qing dynasty. On this typical morning over three hundred years ago, the sun has not yet come up and it is still dark, but with utmost patience the young man receives a number of high-ranking officials and hears reports from all around China. Regardless of whether the news is good or bad, he asks the officials to give their honest appraisals of the goings-on. Afterward, he retreats to his study for private tutorials with the best teachers in the land. He practices calligraphy, painting, horseback riding, and archery. Then, from afternoon until evening, he takes leisurely strolls through beautiful gardens. Servants present him with exquisite delicacies to eat, and musicians play lively music for his pleasure. Later, he honors his ancestors at an altar by lighting incense and bowing to them, asking for their protection.

All these activities took place on a typical day within the imperial palaces known collectively as the Forbidden City. Without doubt, this was a truly forbidding place, made up of imposing gold-tiled buildings, vermilion pillars and gates, and white marble staircases, which all glittered in the sun like a magical land from a fairy tale. Dragons were everywhere: embroidered onto the emperor's robes, carved into his throne, and painted curling up pillars—there was simply no way to count the sheer number of dragons depicted within the Forbidden City. The emperor believed that he himself was a dragon, the ruler of both the palace and the entire land.

Twenty-four emperors resided in the Forbidden City over a period of more than five hundred years. Then eighty years ago, the last emperor, Xuantong, lost the imperial throne and was cast out of the Forbidden City, which was eventually to become known as the Palace Museum, the largest museum in the world.

Should you come to visit, you will see where the emperors passed their daily lives, where they were married, and all sorts of precious curios that they collected. However, when you do come to the Palace Museum, be sure to bring a good map of the grounds, lest you become lost in the maze; wear comfortable walking shoes, as the expanse of the grounds will surpass your imagination; and last but not least, bring a camera. Otherwise, I bet if you try to tell your friends afterward about the mind-boggling grandeur you've seen here, no one will believe you, even when they see the amazed, animated look on your face.

Li Ji
Executive Deputy Director
The Palace Museum
March 15, 2007

OPPOSITE: The Gate of Supreme Harmony, which leads to the Hall of Supreme Harmony and the emperor's golden throne.

PREVIOUS PAGE: The plaza before the Gate of Heavenly Purity, which leads to the imperial family's residential palaces.

A portrait of Yongle, builder of the Forbidden City, capturing his brilliant and sometimes cruel temperament.

OPPOSITE: The phoenix is a mythological bird often shown flying with wings tilted up. Can you see the outline of a soaring wing in the roofline of the Meridian, or Wu men Gate, the main outer gate to the Forbidden City?

Yongle and the Forbidden City

EMPEROR YONGLE, R. 1403–1424

"The enormous walled palace-city within the vast, walled fortress-capital of Peking was truly the Great Within, the inner core ... to which the world beyond was barbarian ..."
—Frank Dorn

For more than two thousand years, China was ruled by powerful families, or dynasties. When one dynasty's power waned, another dynasty would rise up to seize control of this vast country that once stretched from Europe in the west to the East China Sea, as far north as Siberia, and south into what is now Vietnam. It was in this way that the great Ming dynasty began in 1368, when a charismatic peasant named Zhu Yuanzhang led a rebellion against the ruling family of the Yuan dynasty and named himself emperor of China. For the next thirty years, he proved to be a good administrator as well as soldier, introducing new crops, supporting the arts, and sending expeditions as far as Africa. In 1403, his fourth and favorite son, Yongle, seized power from Zhu Yuanzhang's unpopular successor. Fierce, determined Yongle, known as the Black Dragon, was responsible for commissioning one of the most famous structures in the world, a vast complex of more than eight thousand rooms that took fourteen years to build, required the labor of perhaps a million men, and took the lives of thousands of them before its completion. This enormous palace-city would later be called the Forbidden City, because no one, on pain of death, was allowed to enter it without permission.

The idea for the Forbidden City came when Yongle, who had spent much of his youth patrolling the northern borders of China against Mongol invaders, decided to move his government from the city of Nanjing in the south to the city of Peking (now Beijing) in the north. ("Nanjing" means "southern capital," and "Peking" means "northern capital.") There the air was drier, the winds stronger, and the sky so big it looked like the dome of heaven. It was just the spot for Yongle's new city, the one his tutor, a mystic, had envisioned in a dream. There he would build a suitable home for the "Son of Heaven," the one person in the world who, according to Chinese belief, could ask for blessings from heaven for the people of China. The emperor was a religious figure as well as a ruler, and one way he could show this supreme power to his people was to rule from the largest, grandest city in the world, the earthly counterpart to the realm of heaven.

The emperor's city had 980 buildings, and many of them were called palaces or halls. In addition, there were theaters, kitchens, storehouses, gardens, gatehouses, pavilions, and private living spaces.

The city *had* to be large. Ten thousand people lived in it. It had to be strong—so strong that no army, especially the nearby Mongols, would be able invade and conquer it. Yongle built the walls around the city 30 feet high and 30 feet thick. The moat around it was, in some places, 165 feet wide and 20 feet deep. There were only four ways to enter, through enormous gates, each crowned with towering gatehouses. The southern half held grand public spaces while the northern part contained private palaces and courtyards for daily life. Most of the many rooms in the Forbidden City faced south as a protection against the cold winds and evil spirits that came from the north. The north-facing rooms were where disobedient servants were sent to spend the night, shivering with cold and fear.

Leading to the city was a road that passed through the sections of Peking, through the walled Chinese, or outer, city to the south, into the walled Tartar City, where most civil servants lived, then through the Gate of Heavenly Peace into the Imperial City, where high-ranking officials resided. At last, like a jewel hidden inside many boxes, lay the Forbidden City. When an emperor wanted to impress a visitor, he had this three-mile road covered with golden sand. Why would he go to all this trouble? Because at the end of the road was the Hall of Supreme Harmony, and in that hall was a massive golden throne. The emperor was the only one allowed to sit on the throne. When he did, gowned in brilliant silk, on top of tiers of marble and surrounded by golden dragons and towering columns, he indeed looked like the most powerful and well connected person in the world.

Of course, the emperor needed many people to care for him and his family. He needed cooks and tailors, shoemakers and artists, servants and tutors, carpenters and advisers, and priests and monks. Yongle could do very little for himself as he, like the emperors before and after him, believed long, uncut fingernails represented power and high social status. His three-inch nails made simple tasks difficult. One group of people were especially helpful to the emperor and also held considerable power of their own: the eunuchs. These were men who had been castrated, or had their testicles cut off. The eunuchs were the only grown men other than the emperor and his family who were allowed to spend the night in the Forbidden City. At nightfall, the huge gates were shut to all other males. In this way, the emperor tried to ensure that any children born to his many wives and concubines, or mistresses, were his own.

This is just the beginning of the story of the city started by Yongle back in 1407. Over the next five hundred years, twenty-four emperors ruled from this place until the last, young Puyi, fled the city in 1924. In this book you will meet some of the residents and visitors to the city over its long history, and see life within its hidden spaces through their eyes. All are true stories, or based on events that really happened in the magnificent and mysterious Forbidden City.

The Golden Throne as it looks today. Imagine walking three miles on golden sand to reach the emperor, sitting high on this throne.

OPPOSITE: The vast courtyard in front of the Hall of Supreme Harmony in the early-morning hours.

The Story of Emperor Zhengde
and the Palace of Cloudless Heaven

EMPEROR ZHENGDE, R. 1505–1521

"…build the hall again, more beautiful than before. Fill it with treasures more valuable and more beautiful than those that have been lost."

—Emperor Zhengde

Emperor Zhengde had spent thousands of silver coins on the Feast of Lanterns, the final New Year's celebration. He looked around him, dizzy with pride. Surely, no emperor before him had done so much to celebrate the New Year. He had built a seven-story pagoda and draped it with thousands of candles and tiny lanterns, making it look as if it were a fiery constellation floating in the heavens. Hundreds more lanterns danced on the trees: lanterns of lacquer; lanterns of eggshell; lanterns of silk; lanterns made from the horns of water buffalo, scraped and sanded smooth, then boiled, shaped, and painted with the characters for "happiness" and "longevity."

RIGHT: A lantern much like the ones found in the Forbidden City. Today, most lanterns are wired for electricity.

OPPOSITE: Celebrations in the Forbidden City were lavish. This is an emperor's birthday party, but it looks much like the Feast of Lanterns must have looked. Can you find the lanterns, the food, the banners, and the drum?

Fish, in cauldrons of water by a gate or doorway, waited and swam, swam and waited, flashing gold in the light from the lanterns. Fish were the symbol for abundance and, tonight, Zhengde would dazzle the world with the abundance of China.

He was certain he would be remembered as the most generous, the most loved, the richest emperor China had ever had. And now he gazed down from the Golden Throne, craving more . . .

Was an evil spirit from the Gobi desert watching Zhengde? A sudden windstorm swept in from the north. A candle turned into a torch, flames landing on the ladies' brilliant silk gowns. The women threw their long bamboo poles to the ground—poles that held more lanterns—and fled. Fires from the lanterns swept through the rooms like a churning river and threw sparks onto the old wooden rafters of the palace. The guards ran; the musicians ran; the guests ran.

The Palace of Cloudless Heaven burned, burned to the ground.

Zhengde is considered one of the worst emperors in Chinese history. His main interest was pleasure, and, in pursuit of it, he left the governing of China to his eunuchs, who became wealthy buying and selling public offices and taxing the people excessively. Zhengde often traveled, in disguise, throughout his empire and tortured or killed officials he heard speaking out against him. Now, several hundred years later, his reign is still referred to as "an era of disaster."

Zhengde rebuilt the Palace of Cloudless Heaven, within the Forbidden City, in 1516, making it even more lavish than before. It was the heart of court life for more than one hundred years. But the great palace, later renamed the Palace of Surpassing Brightness, was destined to burn again. Angry over years of greedy rulers who lived luxuriously and gave little thought to the harsh lives of their taxpaying subjects, peasants tore down the Palace of Surpassing Brightness and set the rubble on fire. The looting and destruction spread to the outer buildings. Hundreds of servants fled, grabbing priceless gold and jewels on their way out of the massive gates. While much of the Forbidden City remained standing, the Palace of Surpassing Brightness was destroyed.

The rebellion occurred during the reign of Chongzhen (r. 1628–1644). He may have regretted the excesses of his reign, but it was too late. The last Ming emperor turned to his empress and said, "Now the great event is over." His wife, daughter, and concubines committed suicide or were killed. His sons fled. With his favorite eunuch, the emperor walked to the Pavilion of Imperial Longevity on Coal Hill, a hill built to keep out the evil spirits from the north. He wore one red slipper and a long blue gown. On the gown, he wrote, "Because my virtues are insignificant and my personality wretched, I have incurred the wrath of heaven. Hide my face in my hair, let rebels cut my body to pieces, but let them touch not one of my people."

Then he and his faithful eunuch hanged themselves.

Today Coal Hill, where Chongzhen hanged himself, is called Prospect Hill. This is how it looks from the Gate of Divine Prowess at the northern end of the Forbidden City.

OPPOSITE: The Chinese words for "fish" and "abundance" are connected in Chinese culture, thus fish symbolize abundance, or wealth.

The Story of Kangxi and His Elephants

EMPEROR KANGXI, R. 1662–1723

"Like court officials, each elephant was granted a title of nobility in an imperial rescript, at the reading of which the beast knelt respectfully and appeared to listen."

—Frank Dorn

The great elephant stood motionless. Only his ears twitched as his keeper fastened, with leather straps and ropes of silk, a priceless porcelain vase to his head and another to a saddle on his back. The elephant tried to stand still—to not shift his weight, or throw his trunk over his back. He was old and a little cranky. He had seen so many pageants and parades, ceremonies and celebrations. Today, he would have rather stayed in his stall, huge and solid, with walls six feet thick and a deep trench around the edge, where his keeper could find safety in case the elephant turned on him in anger or fear.

But today the bells were ringing, the bells of "goings-out and comings-in." Today the great drum in Phoenix Tower broke through the chatter. For today Emperor Kangxi, the Son of Heaven, would leave the Great Within to visit the Temple of Heaven. Today he would petition the Heavens for a good harvest and blessings on his people.

The elephant led the way toward the Meridian Gate. Dust filled the air as the long procession of elephants stepped in place behind him. When they reached the gate, the elephants formed two lines, making a wide pathway for the emperor. They held their trunks high, as they had been trained, for the long hours it took the procession to pass.

Twenty-four drummers with huge painted drums,
Twenty-four trumpeters playing a song,

OPPOSITE: The ceremonial elephants in the Forbidden City were called "treasured elephants" because of the treasures, such as this large vase, they carried on their elegant saddles. Notice the jewels on the harness and the brilliant silk cloth hanging down the elephant's side.

FOLLOWING PAGE: Drummers, trumpeters, soldiers, eunuchs, flag bearers, and elephants wait for the signal for the almost two-mile-long procession out of the Forbidden City to start. Only the emperor will leave through the center opening, reserved for his exclusive use.

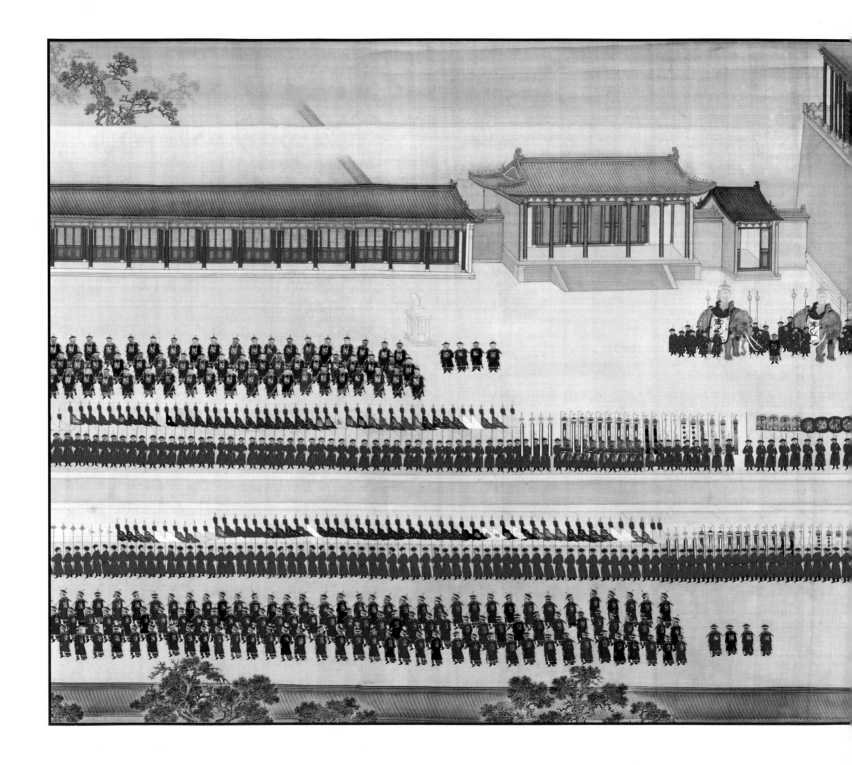

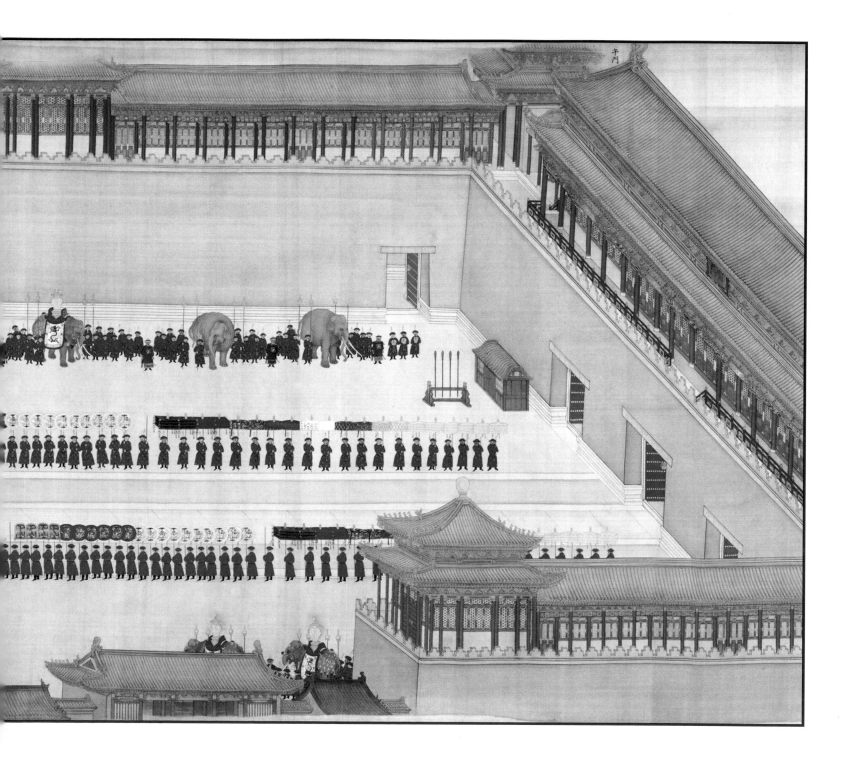

Twenty-four marchers with red-lacquered poles,
One hundred soldiers with crescent-shaped swords,
Four hundred servants with lanterns held high,
Four hundred more their torches ablaze,
Two hundred soldiers, swords trimmed with
    wolves' tails,
Two hundred more with moon and star flags,
Then dancing along, a group of young men,
Balancing a basin and a pitcher of gold,
A silken towel and objects untold
(For who knows what the emperor might need?).
Next pranced ten white horses,
Decked with pearls and jewels,
Followed by lancers, one hundred more,
Five hundred princes,
Nobles,
And royals,
One thousand eunuchs, richly red gowned,
And four thousand soldiers marching along.
All to honor the emperor, as he spoke to the heavens
For harvest and health,
And good fortune for all.

The elephant lowered his trunk. The last flowing robe,
jeweled horse, and brilliant flag had passed. He plodded back
to his stall. Maybe there would be new hay, a cabbage or ten,
and great mounds of fruit. For today he had watched over the
emperor and kept him safe.

Replicas of elephants, such as this jade elephant trinket, capturing the elephant's power and quiet wisdom, are a vital part of Chinese culture today.

OPPOSITE: A faithful bronze elephant rests in the Forbidden City's Imperial Garden.

Riding on an elephant symbolizes *ji-xiang*, or happiness.

OPPOSITE: The Temple of Heaven, south of the Forbidden City, is the largest complex in the world designed for worship. It was built in 1420 by Emperor Yongle.

Kangxi was one of China's three great Manchu emperors, of the Qing dynasty. The Qing emperors were descended from invaders who came out of the northeast, beyond the Great Wall that protected the northern border of China, and conquered the Ming dynasty. Born in the Forbidden City in 1654, Kangxi became emperor at age eight after his father's death. Four regents helped him rule until he was twelve, when he married, dismissed the regents, and assumed full power. For the next sixty-one years, Kangxi ruled wisely and well. He developed the agricultural system, supported and practiced the arts, published encyclopedias and dictionaries, used diplomacy or force to establish peace with warring peoples, and spread the teachings of Confucius, a philosopher who lived over a thousand years before Kangxi and who left many writings about living a life of charity, justice, and truth.

On the day of the elephant-guarded procession, Kangxi was leaving the Forbidden City for the Temple of Heaven, located south of the Forbidden City, to perform the annual Plowing Ceremony. As mediator between Heaven and Earth, the emperor was entrusted with rituals that, according to tradition, would keep his people safe and healthy. Once he reached the Temple of Heaven, he fasted, meditated, prayed, and then, with high-ranking ministers, plowed the first three furrows of the year. According to tradition, farmers could now plow and plant their fields as officially "all plants could bud and grow."

As emperors had for a thousand years before him, Kangxi kept elephants in his court as symbols of strength. The emperors' elephants were so loved, they were given the titles of nobility and lived in great luxury. Elephants are still much loved in China today.

The Story of Emperor Qianlong and the Breakfast Party Guest

EMPEROR QIANLONG (GRANDSON OF KANGXI), R. 1736–1796

"Having had so near a view of the emperor of China this morning, it seems natural that I should say something of the person and dress."

—André Everard Van Braam Houckgeest

The emperor was often carried in a palanquin similar to this one. He was always followed by a procession of servants, carrying dishes of food, just in case he became hungry.

OPPOSITE: The lion was the symbol for bravery and might in ancient China. Today, lions and lion pairs guard shops, banks, restaurants, government buildings, and even schools. This one has his foot on a ball, telling everyone he represents imperial power.

January 20, 1795

I, André Everard Van Braam Houckgeest, envoy from the Dutch East India Company, am entering the Forbidden City through the Gate of Western Glory. It is one of only three ways visitors may enter the city. My servants carry my sedan chair, shoulder high, until we reach the inner gate. From there, I must walk, bearing my cushion, jostling others on the path. I can't be late for the emperor's breakfast.

At last I reach the vast marble courtyard, covered with a sea of thick carpets. I sit on my cushion, waiting, brushing the snow off my robe.

Quick, everyone must stand! Emperor Qianlong is coming. We hear the soft music of cymbals and flutes that announce his arrival. Bearers carry his golden chair through the Wu men, or the Noon, Gate, the gate for the emperors only, who have the power of the noonday sun. We all want a glimpse of him.

When he passes, I am close enough to see that his silk robes are lined with otter fur, his beard is gray, and on his cap is one large pearl. I fall on my knees and bow three times in the salute of honor, the first of many I will give.

Servants carry him down the Imperial Way, and over a marble ramp leading into the Hall of Supreme Harmony. On either side bronze lions sit at attention, guarding the Hall as they have done for centuries, for just inside, on a platform six feet high, is the Golden Throne.

We cannot eat until the emperor has tasted from the dishes placed before him. We cannot drink until the emperor has sipped from the cup of wine.

On the table I share with others are rows and rows of fine porcelain dishes filled with fragrant rice, steamed cakes, fried puff-pastry, and twice-seasoned soup. Boiled legs of mutton rest in great copper kettles. When at last we may eat, drums beat and bells chime and dancers swirl around us. I taste a bit from each bowl, drink some wine, and hold my robe close to me in the cold.

Finally, it is my turn to enter the hall and approach the Golden Throne. Emperor Qianlong hands me a cup of wine. I must bow low, while holding the wine with both hands. I cannot take my hat off as I kneel and touch my forehead to the carpet. Plop! My hat has fallen off my head! Emperor Qianlong laughs.

"Do you not understand Chinese?" he asks.

I try to say "budong," to indicate I do not know much about the language, but it comes out as "poton."

This makes him laugh more. His skin is wrinkled, his beard is thin and gray, but his eyes are filled with kindness.

Emperor Qianlong carried on the tradition of his grandfather, Kangxi, for the sixty years of his reign, devoting himself to expanding and improving the agriculture, crafts, and culture of China. New crops, such as corn and sweet potato, were introduced during his reign. He encouraged the production of silks, ceramics, paper, and porcelain, and shipped them by sea to markets in the West.

During the time of Qianlong's reign, and until the early nineteenth century, the Chinese had little exposure to the rest of the world. Jesuit missionaries were tolerated and Western diplomats and representatives of trading companies, such as Houckgeest, were allowed entry. But the emperors closely guarded the activities of foreigners in China. As Sons of Heaven, the Chinese emperors believed themselves superior to the "foreign devils" or "barbarians."

They also were worried that China could be taken over. China's exposure to the West remained closely controlled until the Opium War—a war that started over the smuggling of a drug called opium—was lost to the British in 1842. This weakened the rule of the emperors and started China's economic, political, and social change.

However, for almost fifty years after Qianlong's rule, China held to its old ways. The Golden Throne was still the symbolic center of power, and visitors to the court still had to walk across the vast marble courtyard, as big as 155 tennis courts, to reach the emperor. The emperor was carried over a hallowed section called the Dragon Pavement, a tiered platform more than twenty-four feet high. The tiers were decorated with carvings of dragons and phoenixes, the symbols for the emperor and empress. The center stairway was the "spirit stairway," white marble carved with dragons and clouds. Bearers carried the emperor over this very carefully. If they stepped on this sacred walk, they could be executed!

LEFT: More than one thousand fierce-looking dragon heads hang from the sides of buildings in the Forbidden City, as symbols of the emperor. A row of stone dragons hangs from a wall leading to the Hall of Central Harmony (behind the Hall of Supreme Harmony). When it rained, water streamed off the roofs and through the dragons' mouths.

OPPOSITE: The Dragon Pavement is carved from one huge block of marble. It took twenty-thousand workers and a thousand mules to drag the stone thirty miles to the Forbidden City. This was done during the cold of winter, so the workers could splash water on the road and slide the stone over the ice that formed.

The throne hall rose above other buildings in the Forbidden City. Each pillar supporting the roof was a giant tree, cut and dragged from a forest hundreds of miles away. Large incense burners decorated with mythological animal figures stood like sentries on the platform. They were said to be the emperor's eyes, and with them he could see all corners of his kingdom. In the center was the Golden Throne. The massive platform, the carvings, the gargoyles, the very size of the throne, all had the effect of striking awe into the hearts of the emperor's visitors, especially diplomats from far-off countries. He must have looked like the Son of Heaven indeed.

The Story of Emperor Qianlong in the Pavilion for Bestowing Wine

"The imperial fairyland . . . where the burdens of state could be forgotten among ancient trees, delicate flowers, and time-worn rocks."

—Wan-go Weng and Yang Boda

It is the third day of the third month. Emperor Qianlong and his friends have gathered in a small courtyard called the Pavilion for Bestowing Wine. Qianlong watches as the sun plays with the water in the stream that winds through the courtyard. He marks its rhythm as it laps against the stones and gurgles with the current. He listens to the wind as it moves through the trees, where the nightingale sings.

A servant gently sets a goblet of wine on the drifting water. It bobs, then rights itself, and starts on its journey, turning and following the stream's bends. Qianlong and his friends hush their murmurs and watch the cup. Where will it stop?

There, it has caught in a turn in front of Qianlong. The emperor leans over the water and plucks out the cup. Raising it up, he closes his eyes. All is silent, even the nightingale. When he speaks, his voice is that of an old man, quavering, but still commanding:

". . . a pavilion a path, a pace a scene,
the scene changes with each pace,
and each pace is of great interests."

Emperor Qianlong and his children are relaxing in a garden. The painting is full of symbols: The crane stands for longevity, the mandarin ducks in the lotus pond stand for happiness in a marriage, and the willow tree wards off demons.

OPPOSITE: The Wine-Cup-Floating Stream in the garden of the Pavilion of the Ceremony for Purification.

Qianlong and his friends honor an ancient custom. On the third day of the third month of each year, they gather in this courtyard and watch the cup float and bob, around and around, until it stops, caught on a branch or rock in the stream. The person it stops in front of must think of a poem and recite it to the others, then place the cup back in the water, until it finds the next person who also has "ink in his stomach," which means he, too, finds quiet joy in poetry.

The Ten-Thousand-Springs Pavilion is part of the Imperial Garden. The yellow flowers, which bloom first, are meant to welcome spring. In the background is a cypress tree, a symbol for longevity.

Out of respect for his grandfather, Kangxi, who reigned for sixty-one years, Qianlong turned his power over to his son in his sixtieth year as emperor. This is part of his last official speech:

> I have now reigned for fifty-nine years. By the favor of high Heaven and the protection of my ancestors, peace prevails throughout my dominions, and new territories have come to share the blessings of China's civilization. During those years I have striven to alleviate my people's lot and show myself worthy of Heaven's blessings . . . [I] came to the Throne in early childhood . . . today I am eighty-four . . . I rejoice in the possession of perfect health, and my descendants to the fourth generation surround me . . .

Most likely, Qianlong spent many happy hours after his abdication in the Forbidden City gardens. Gardens were the one place where the emperors could rest and reflect, or find inspiration for their poetry, music, and painting. Hidden behind walls and tucked between palaces and public spaces, each garden was an oasis of peace and calm in an otherwise busy city.

Official duties in the Forbidden City were conducted in the early morning, often before the sun was up. Later in the day, emperors found a sheltered spot in a favorite garden to paint, practice calligraphy, or write poetry, typically about the beauty of nature. Sometimes they would play a musical instrument such as a lute or a zither. Music from lutes was thought to be sweet and elegant, happy and sad, a mix of many things in life.

TOP: Ancient trees, sometimes hundreds of years old, were loved by most emperors. Some trees were even made part of the noble class and given a title such as duke or lord.

BOTTOM: A young woman wearing a traditional silk jacket holds a replica of an ancient stringed instrument.

The Story of Dowager Princess Su's Funeral

LIFE OF PRINCESS SU, MID 1800S–DATE UNKNOWN

"It is a comfort to us to get and send her everything she liked while she lived, and it helps us bear our sorrows."

—Third daughter of the dowager princess to Mrs. Headland

Who are these people crowding my palace? Why are they wearing rough white sacks instead of silken robes?

Ah . . . now I remember. I was taken from them. I was old and sick. I lived well, and now these people are saying good-bye . . . to me. I'll hover and keep watch, and tell you what I see.

A heavy yellow curtain covers the door leading to the altar in the sacrificial room where my guests kneel on rope matting and wail, foreheads touching the floor. Yellow, the color of the imperial family. I was married to a prince of one of the Eight Great Families chosen to help the emperors of the Qing dynasty. I had children, born high and noble. Now my daughters and granddaughters kneel on the rope matting that covers the floor.

People are starting to leave this small room. I follow them to the courtyard, covered by a canopy and filled with heavy silk banners. The writing on each banner proclaims my virtues. My friends made these banners. How could they have so much to say about me?

Now, for the fun part. The feast! The presents! A veranda has been built, five feet wide and forty feet long and covered with towers of fruit and cakes, food for my spirit. I hear priests chanting and music coming from small horns and drums as we all walk into the street for the great bonfire—the burning of the gifts, my presents for the afterlife.

There is a carriage pulled by horses, a chair like the one I was carried in, a big house, servants, money, flowers, and my playing cards and dice, for I loved games. All are made of paper and all will be burned, and the flames will send my gifts into the spirit world—to me.

LEFT: The altar in the niche on the third floor of the Pavilion of the Rain of Flowers in the Forbidden City, part of the northern Inner Court where the emperors and their families lived.

OPPOSITE, TOP: A row of life-size paper horses will be burned at a modern-day Chinese funeral. Because the horses are large and many in number, the dead person most likely was wealthy and had a strong interest in what they represent.

OPPOSITE, BOTTOM: On Qingming, an annual day for honoring the dead, relatives buy small paper boxes to burn in the temples in remembrance of their dead.

This is a typical altar to Buddha, laden with food and incense on Qingming.

OPPOSITE, TOP: A young boy lights incense to honor his grandmother on Qingming.

OPPOSITE, BOTTOM: A woman folds a small silver box that will be thrown into the fire on Qingming at Jade Buddha Temple in Shanghai.

Princess Su's funeral was typical for someone of her family's rank and importance in China. When the Qing dynasty officially started in 1644, the emperor, named Shunzhi, honored Eight Great Families who had helped him establish his rule. The men of the families were made noblemen and called Iron Caps. Princess Su's ancestors were one of these families. They did not live inside the Forbidden City, but in the southern part of the Tartar City, which surrounded the Forbidden City.

Many customs at Princess Su's funeral are still practiced in China today. Mourners at funerals often wear clothes made from *su*, or unbleached sackcloth (really more of a beige color than the white sacks Princess Su describes). Gold and silver paper is folded into small boxes, called *jin ming* and *yin ming*, that will be burned at the grave, sending wealth to the deceased. Other paper gifts are made, replicas of the objects that gave the deceased comfort in life, such as a special chair or playing cards. Mourners file to the graveyard, where they set up a small banquet on a slab of stone—fish and meat dishes, rice, cooked vegetables, fresh fruit, a sweet, and a bottle of wine. A plate and cup and a pair of chopsticks are put by the food while the boxes are burned. Firecrackers are lit, for luck. When the mourners leave, some food is left behind for the deceased.

Every year on April 5, the Chinese celebrate Qingming, or "bright and shining day." This is the one day a year they officially pay respects to their dead, visiting grave sites, pulling weeds, and sweeping the stones clean. They perform rituals in a temple and celebrate life with walks in the park in the warm spring weather.

The Story of Empress Dowager Cixi in Her Private Rooms

EMPRESS DOWAGER CIXI, 1862–1908 (IN POWER)

"The Current Holy Mother Empress Dowager Cixi Duanyou Kangyi Zhaoyu Zhuangcheng Shougong Qinxian Chongxi of the Great Qing Empire"
—Official name for Cixi at her death

Empress Dowager Cixi wakes up in her palace in the Forbidden City. She gazes at the handscroll hanging opposite her bed. In delicate colors, the artist has painted on silk a fenghuang, *or* phoenix, *a large, mythological bird that represents peace and prosperity. Light is just starting to come in through the window looking over the garden. Cixi stretches.*

As empress dowager, she ruled China for over forty years, but last year she turned power over to her nephew. Now she can sleep until dawn, instead of waking at three in the morning to start her duties. Now she is known as Master Old Buddha.

Her bed is a platform against a wall, with three tall sides made of carved wood. Her mattress is covered with yellow satin, her sheets are yellow silk, and her quilt is yellow satin embroidered with dragons. Yellow curtains surround the bed. Yellow is the color of royalty, and only royalty and Buddhist monks are allowed to wear it—or sleep under it.

The small bed stays warm from the heated bricks beneath it. Cixi shuts her eyes. She would like to stay behind her closed yellow curtains just a little longer, but her servants are waiting to start the day.

Some say that the phoenix has the face of a swallow, the neck of a snake, the back of a tortoise, and the tail of a fish.

OPPOSITE: Cixi's bedroom in a palace in the Forbidden City. A picture of a phoenix, the symbol for the empress, hangs on the wall. The emperor's symbol is the dragon.

大清國慈禧皇太后

Notice Cixi's long nails and the jade bracelets she is wearing. Pearls and jade were her favorite jewelry. The characters on her gown stand for longevity. Her hairstyle and headdress were typical for Manchu women.

She touches the curtain. She does not need to say anything—a servant calls for hot milk. Another pours warm water into the basin; a third stands ready with a towel. Two more servants wait outside her inner door. Four more sit by a red lacquered outer door, and a dozen more are waiting nearby. Cixi has little privacy.

When she has bathed, she chooses a gown from the thousands she owns, all packed in yellow silk. Next she picks jewelry from the six hundred boxes that line the walls of a room next to her bedroom. Today she wears a string of fat pearls in her hair, gold and jade bracelets, and a sapphire and ruby pin made to look like a dragonfly. A servant combs and braids her hair, and the empress rubs perfumed cream into her skin. She is ready to leave her private rooms and start her public day. Twenty-four servants follow the chair she is riding in, to one of the great audience halls. Each is carrying something—comb and shoes, perfumes and pins, handkerchiefs, brushes, powder, and paper. She brings her dressing room with her! Who knows what a busy empress might need?

Empress Dowager Cixi had many names, but by the end of her long life, she was simply known as Master Old Buddha.

At age sixteen, Cixi, a Manchu from the northern plains, entered the court as a concubine to Emperor Xianfeng (r. 1851–1861). Luckily for Cixi, she gave birth to his only son, which gave her a chance to use her considerable abilities to gain great power in the court. When her son died as a young man, Cixi's nephew, Guangxu, officially became emperor. Although it was Guangxu who sat on the Golden Throne, curious and controlling Cixi sat very close, behind a yellow screen, so she could listen to everything that was being said. It was she who made the state decisions during both her son's and her nephew's reigns. Briefly, she turned over control to her nephew, then quickly took it back when he made decisions she didn't like.

Empress Dowager Cixi lived in one of the six palaces in the northwestern part of the Forbidden City, protected from the public southern spaces by walls and gardens and screens. She filled her rooms with sweet-smelling flowers, such as peach blossoms, which were believed to keep demons at bay and to increase longevity. A hidden stairway in the bedroom led to a Buddhist chapel, where the empress prayed. She also received guests in these rooms. When the wives of diplomats from the West paid her a visit, she changed almost everything in her room—the curtains, the bedcovers, the wall decorations, the vases—and changed it back again when they left, not wanting strangers to become familiar with this private space.

She also received them in great finery. She chose earrings, bracelets, necklaces, and jeweled hairpins to go with her robe. She even wore jeweled shoes. And because emperors and empresses believed long fingernails were a symbol of their high social status, Cixi protected the nails on her third and fourth fingers with golden nail shields embedded with rubies, jade, and pearls.

TOP: Cixi's grave is outside the Forbidden City. She planned well for her death, ordering an elaborate tomb. Look closely at the picture of the walkway leading to her grave. Can you see the phoenix and the dragon? Cixi planned this, too. She was so powerful, she ordered that this slab of marble be carved with the dragon *underneath* the phoenix, which was against all tradition. The dragon was the symbol for the emperor, the most powerful and mystical person in the world!

BOTTOM: Cixi's most beautiful headdresses were said to be made from the tiny feathers found on a kingfisher's breast, or from the delicate wings of a butterfly. Young women in China still enjoy being photographed in elaborate headdresses of the type Cixi wore.

The Story of
The Last Emperor,
Xuantong

EMPEROR XUANTONG
(BETTER KNOWN AS PUYI), R. 1908–1911

"When a pupil meets his teacher on the road, he should bow ... as long as his teacher lives he must serve him zealously, and should pay him the tribute of sincere mourning for three years after his death ..."

—The *Li chi*, a book of Confucian teachings

Puyi peeked out from behind the yellow silk curtains around his palanquin, the raised chair in which his servants carried him from palace to palace. Today the sky was the color of a sapphire. The breeze swept away the heavy air inside the curtains. If only the eunuchs carrying my chair were sturdy ponies, *he thought.* I would kick them with my feet and we would gallop out the northern gate. I would ride the northern plains and not stop until I was tired. I would drink from waterfalls, and sleep counting the stars.

Like the Qing emperors before him, Puyi was a Manchu, one of the fierce people who lived on the northern plains of China. On days like this, with the fragrant air calling him, he longed for freedom and adventure.

Puyi had been the emperor of China since he was two years and ten months old. His father was his regent, which meant he ruled until Puyi was old enough to do so. China had been taken over by the army when Puyi was three, but he still lived inside the walls of the Forbidden City, with only eunuchs and servants to keep him company.

As a young boy, Puyi never left the Forbidden City. It is said he didn't see another child until he was seven years old. His head was full of lessons, just in case the Imperial Court was restored to power.

Puyi closed the curtains to his palanquin. He was thirteen, and today he would start learning English. He must remember his manners for his new tutor, and be open to Western ways so he can lead his country into the modern world.

The tutor was early—no one was late for meeting with the emperor. He waited for his pupil in the Palace of the Bringing-Forth-of-Blessings, or the imperial schoolroom, sipping tea.

Chao! *cried a eunuch, startling the new tutor.*

Puyi stood in the doorway.

Chao! *cried another eunuch.*

This was the signal that classes could begin. Puyi sat facing south, his back to the evil forces of the north. His tutor faced west. Puyi studied English, the Manchu language, poetry, and calligraphy, for "uncut jade cannot be turned into a serviceable vessel." But all this discipline, all this preparation was for a day that would never come. Puyi's future lay outside the city of emperors.

TOP: The calligraphy that Puyi studied is still practiced today and is often used for invitations to special events or to write poetry.

BOTTOM: This young boy is wearing yellow, a color once forbidden to all but the emperors and monks. On his coat is a dragon, symbol of the emperor. Perhaps he is pretending to be the emperor.

OPPOSITE: Puyi as a teenager wearing traditional silk clothing.

Puyi would not be trapped inside the Forbidden City forever. Great change had come to China and its last emperor's life would change also. After the Taiping Rebellion, a bloody revolt against the Qing government that killed millions, and a difficult war with Japan, the Imperial Court was weakened and no longer had the power to rule China. In 1911, the military took over and the country was declared a republic with a constitution and a president. Puyi, only three years old at the time, was allowed to continue living in the Forbidden City. It was best for the people in power if he stayed inside the walled city, away from those who might help him regain his throne. When Puyi realized that he was, in effect, being jailed in the Forbidden City, he bribed the guards and tried to escape, but they kept the money and did not help him. At age eighteen, he was forced out of the Forbidden City by a warlord and sent to Japan, then to Manchuria, where he was made a "puppet" emperor under the control of the Japanese. He was later exiled to Russia, where he was kept a prisoner in a guarded but comfortable house.

In 1950 he returned to China and was forced to work in a prison camp. This was when he finally turned over the great imperial seal, the symbol of the emperor's power. In 1959, he was released. Finally, Puyi lived as an ordinary citizen.

Although he was still a puppet, used by others for power, for the first time in his life he was relatively free to come and go as he pleased. He lived in Beijing, married, got a job as gardener, and became a devout Buddhist. "I had no freedom as emperor," he is reported to have said, "but now I have found my freedom."

The color yellow was reserved for use by the emperor and monks, and most things in Puyi's world were yellow—his bedding, his dishes, the floors he walked on, his robes. There is a story that says he was once enraged as a child when he glimpsed the yellow lining of his cousin's sleeve. Today anyone can wear yellow. Yellow is an especially popular color for small replicas of the emperor's hat, such as the one worn by this young boy.

OPPOSITE: When Puyi left the Forbidden City for the last time, he walked through the Shenwumen Gate, the northern gate. The Meridian Gate, opening to the south, was the gate of emperors. In leaving by the less important northern gate, used by servants and tradesmen, this earnest young man with round spectacles and a head full of lessons, may have been signaling the beginning of a very different, private life.

Epilogue

A young girl sits on a replica of the Golden Throne as she checks her cell phone. This small throne is one example of how the artifacts and symbols of the Forbidden City, once used only by the emperor and his family, have filtered down to represent China in a new way.

OPPOSITE: More than eight million people from all over the world visit the Forbidden City each year.

The change that swept through China ended the system of dynasties that had governed the country for the past twenty-five hundred years (five hundred of those years from the Forbidden City). Communism, a type of government in which most property is owned collectively by the state and the people, eventually took its place.

Because of these changes, the psychological and physical barriers protecting the Forbidden City collapsed, and this most powerful symbol of the old ways lost many of its priceless treasures. During the collapse, eunuchs and servants smuggled riches out. Thieves took what they could. A pillow in which a long string of perfect pearls was hidden is said to have been sold to a merchant for the equivalent of one dollar. Do you think he ever found the pearls?

In the decades after the reign of the emperors was over, China became busy rebuilding itself as a new country. One of the new country's early acts was to sort and count the remaining tresaures in the Forbidden City, and, in 1925, to declare the palaces a museum. Today, Yongle's city is still being restored to its former beauty. Many spaces, resplendent in their new coats of red, blue, green, and gold paint, are open to the public. Many more spaces, however, are still behind thick walls, hidden by gnarled trees, the secret rooms and underground passageways holding their stories and their secrets for yet a little longer.

Today, the Forbidden City is a public museum with eight million tourists visiting each year. It is a World Heritage Site, a United Nations designation for places such as the pyramids of Egypt and the Great Barrier Reef in Australia. Being a World Heritage Site means that these places belong to all peoples of the world.

Would the emperors be angry, surprised, shocked, and dismayed to see so many visitors from all over the world in their fortress home? Or would they look upon this reincarnation of their city with wonder and fascination, amusement and pride? If you have the opportunity, go and see the Forbidden City for yourself. Wander through the bays and rooms, the elegant gardens, the halls and courtyards and gates. Imagine the life that ebbed and flowed during the magnificent and extraordinary days when the Forbidden City teemed with eunuchs and concubines, servants and diplomats, imperial families and foreign visitors, elephants and ancient trees, and, of course, one Son of Heaven sitting on a Golden Throne.

The Tai He Gate leading to the emperor's throne in the Hall of Supreme Harmony.

Between dawn and dusk, the red wall stands
From ancient to modern, the magic door links
There is a history which hasn't been devoured
    by time
There is a dream which has lingered for more
    than two hundred years.

—From a plaque in the Forbidden City

TIMELINE OF IMPORTANT DATES AND EMPERORS OF THE FORBIDDEN CITY

551 BCE—birth of Confucius

Confucius was a Chinese philosopher whose ideas about morality and justice affected thought and culture throughout East Asia, far beyond China's borders. His teachings were well known to the inhabitants of the Forbidden City.

221 BCE—Qin Shihuangdi* becomes the first emperor of China

Qin Shihuangdi, a powerful, ruthless leader, is credited with unifying China.

1206 CE—Genghis Khan founds the Mongol Empire

The Mongol Empire, which lasted until 1368, was the largest contiguous empire in world history, as well as the second largest for total landmass. It included China.

1368–1644—MING DYNASTY

1368–1398—reign of Hongwu* [hung'woo] **(Zhu Yuanzhang)** [joo yew'en j'ang]

1398–1402—reign of Tianwen*

1403–1424—reign of Yongle [yung' le]

1425—reign of Hongxi

1426–1435—reign of Xuande

1436–1449—reign of Zhengtong†

1450–1456—reign of Jingtai

1457–1464—reign of Tianshun†

1465–1487—reign of Chenghua

1488–1505—reign of Hongzhi

1505–1521—reign of Zhengde [tch'eng de]

1522–1566—reign of Jiajing

1567–1572— reign of Longqing

1573–1619— reign of Wanli

1620—reign of Taichang

1621–1627—reign of Tianqi

1628–1644—reign of Chongzhen [ch'ong tch'en]

1644–1911—QING DYNASTY

1644–1661—reign of Shunzhi

1662–1723—reign of Kangxi [k'ang tschee]

1723–1735—reign of Yongzheng

1736–1796—reign of Qianlong [tch'ee an long]

1796–1820—reign of Jiaqing

1821–1850—reign of Daoguang

1851–1861—reign of Xianfeng

1862–1874—reign of Tongzhi

1875–1908—reign of Guangxu

Mid 1800s–Date unknown— life of Princess Dowager Su [s'su]

1862–1908—Empress Dowager Cixi [ts'e e tschee] **in power**

1908–1911—reign of Xuantong [schuen t'ong] **(Puyi)** [p'oo ee]

1987—The Forbidden City becomes a World Heritage Site

2008—China hosts the Olympics

* Emperors who predated the Forbidden City
† Separate reigns of the same person

GLOSSARY

Abdication—The act of resigning from a throne or a position of power and leadership.

Bay—A "room" in a Chinese building that is defined as "the space among four pillars."

Buddhist [boo' dist]—A follower of an ancient Eastern religion based on the teachings of an Indian philosopher, living in the fifth century BCE, named Sakyamuni Buddha (566–480 BCE).

Calligraphy [cal lig' ra fee]—Literally, beautiful writing. Skill in calligraphy was an important criterion for being selected to become part of the imperial court in the Forbidden City. It is still considered one of the highest art forms in China.

Cauldron—A large, deep, round iron pot.

Chinese characters—The Chinese language is written in characters, or drawings, that stand for a complete word or phrase. All words are written in these small symbolic pictures instead of in an alphabet system. Although spoken languages in China may differ, written Chinese characters are the same for everyone. Chinese characters are read from top to bottom and from left to right. There are thousands of characters, and a reader needs to know at least three thousand of them to be able to read a newspaper.

Chinese language—Many varieties of the Chinese language, called dialects, are spoken in this very large country, but the official spoken language is Mandarin Chinese.

Concubine [kon' cue bine]—A woman who fills the role of a wife in countries where polygamy is allowed. In the Forbidden City, concubines had a lower social status than empresses. Their status could be considerably improved if they bore the emperor children, particularly sons.

Diplomat—A person sent to another country to foster official and friendly relations.

Dynasty—A line of rulers coming from the same family or hereditary background.

Eunuch [you' nik]—A man who has had his

testicles removed. Eunuchs, because they lacked reproductive organs, helped ensure the legitimacy of children born to the empresses and imperial concubines in the Forbidden City.

Gobi desert [go' bee]—A large desert in Asia, situated north of China, in Mongolia.

Gourd—A fruit, usually round, that has a hard skin or shell.

Incense—A substance, often used in religious ceremonies, that has a strong, sweet smell when burned.

Jade—A hard blue, green, or white stone often used for jewelry, statues, ornaments, and ritual implements.

Mah-Jongg [ma' jawng]—A game of Chinese origin played by four persons with domino-like pieces.

Manchu [man' choo]—A person from an area in what is now northeast China.

Moat—A wide, deep ditch circling a building or complex of buildings.

Mongol [mon' goal]—A nomadic person from what is now Mongolia, a country north of China.

Mythological—Pertaining to myths, or traditional, legendary stories usually associated with unnatural events or superhumans.

Opium [oh' pee um]—A drug made from the juice of poppies.

Pagoda [pa go' da]—A building, often associated with Buddhism, that can have many stories, each marked by an upward-tilted tiered roof or eave.

Palanquin [pal en keen']—A one-person passenger carriage carried by means of poles on the shoulders of the bearers.

Pinyin [pin' yin]—In addition to learning Chinese characters, children in China also learn pinyin, which is a second way of reading and writing words in Chinese. Pinyin uses the alphabet (the same one used in the English language) to write words the way they sound in Mandarin Chinese.

Regent—Someone appointed to rule a country when the real ruler is too young to rule, or is sick or absent.

Reincarnation—A belief that the soul of a dead person can come back in another body.

BIBLIOGRAPHY

Abrams Discoveries. *The Forbidden City: Center of Imperial Power.* New York, NY: Harry N. Abrams, Inc., 1997.

Anderson, Mary M. *Hidden Power: The Palace Eunuchs of Imperial China.* Buffalo, NY: Prometheus Books, 1990.

Der Ling, Princess. *Lotos Petals.* New York, NY: Dodd, Mead & Co., 1930.

————. *Two Years in the Forbidden City.* New York, NY: Moffat, Yard, and Co., 1911.

Dorn, Frank. *The Forbidden City: The Biography of a Palace.* New York, NY: Charles Scribner's Sons, 1970.

Eberhard, Wolfram. *A Dictionary of Chinese Symbols: Hidden Symbols in Chinese Life and Thought.* London: Routledge, 1986.

Headland, Isaac Taylor. *Court Life in China.* New York, NY: F.H. Revell Co., 1909.

Hoff, Rhoda. *China: Adventures in Eyewitness History.* New York, NY: Henry Z. Walck, Inc., 1965.

Johnston, Reginald F. *Twilight in the Forbidden City.* New York, NY: D. Appleton-Century Co., 1934.

Loti, Pierre. *The Last Days of Pekin.* Boston, MA: Little, Brown, and Co., 1902. Translated by Myrta L. Jones.

Mitamura, Taisuke. *Chinese Eunuchs: The Structure of Intimate Politics.* North Clarenden, VT: Tuttle Publishing, 1970. Translated by Charles A. Pomeroy.

Palace Museum. *The Palace Museum.* Beijing: Forbidden City Palace Publishing House, 2006.

Seagrave, Sterling, with Peggy Seagrave. *Dragon Lady: The Life and Legend of the Last Empress of China.* New York, NY: Alfred A. Knopf, 1992.

Varè, Daniele. *The Last Empress.* Garden City, NY: Doubleday, Doran, & Co., Inc., 1936.

Williams, C. A. S. *Chinese Symbolism and Art Motifs.* Boston, MA: Castle Books, Charles E. Tuttle Co., Inc., Boston, 1974.

Yang Xin and Zhu Chengru. *Secret World of the Forbidden City: Splendors from China's Imperial Palace.* Santa Ana, CA: Bowers Museum of Cultural Arts, in conjunction with the Palace Museum, Beijing, China: 2000.

AUTHOR'S NOTE

In telling the history of the Forbidden City, in all its vitality, I chose to write parts of this book from the points of view of historical figures, an elephant, and even a ghost. Each of these seven "stories" is based on accounts of actual events, detailed in the books listed in the bibliography. The reader should also note that the dates of the reigns of the emperors vary from source to source. The dates used throughout come from the official Palace Museum guidebook.

ACKNOWLEDGMENTS

Much cooperation and cross-cultural connection were needed to bring this book into print, so special thanks to the following:

Our friends in China, who answered many questions about Chinese culture and made us welcome: Felix Lee, Joseph Lo, and Ken Lin; our translators: Tianlu, James, Fei Fei, and Andrew; our contacts at the Forbidden City: Zhang Ying, Shaoyi Li, and Si Bing.

For help in establishing contact and getting permission to work with Forbidden City officials: Senator Hillary Clinton and her staff, especially Kris Balderston; Wu Qiang and Han Hong at the Chinese Embassy; and MengHao Zhao.

For vetting the manuscript: Professor Hsin-Mei Agnes Hsu, Andrew W. Mellon Scholar in Chinese Archaeology, Stanford University; James Hargett, Professor of Chinese Studies, State University of New York at Albany; and Nixi Cura, Course Director, Christie's Education, London. Translators Anne McDonough and Adam Ross for their help with the introduction.

In grateful appreciation for our friends at the China Institute in America, especially Kevin Lawrence, for their support and encouragement. Thanks also to Joe Gerena.

And thanks to our editor, Susan Van Metre, who stayed with the project through its many ups and downs in the past three years.

IMAGE CREDITS

Images courtesy of The Palace Museum: pp. 2–3, 4, 6, 7, 8, 9, 10, 13, 14, 16-17, 18, 22, 24, 25, 26, 27, 28, 31, 34, 36, 37 top, 38, 40, 43, 44, 45

Images copyright © Ellen B. Senisi: pp. 11, 12, 19, 21, 23, 29 top, 29 bottom, 30 top, 30 bottom, 32, 33 top, 33 bottom, 35, 37 bottom, 39 top, 39 bottom, 41, 42

Images copyright © Panorama Images / The Image Works: p. 20

CREDITS

Trish Marx: concept, research, text, photo selection, glossary, timeline

Ellen B. Senisi: concept, research, permissions, photography, photo selection, glossary, timeline

For Molly, with love
—TM

For JPS, my photo assistant for this book and partner on the journey
—EBS

Library of Congress Cataloging-in-Publication Data
Marx, Trish.
Elephants and golden thrones : inside China's Forbidden City / by Trish Marx ; photography by Ellen B. Senisi ; foreword by Mr. Li Ji.
p. cm.
ISBN-13: 978-0-8109-9485-0 (hardcover)
ISBN-10: 0-8109-9485-2 (hardcover)
I. Forbidden City (Beijing, China)—Anecdotes—Juvenile literature.
I. Senisi, Ellen B. II. Title. III. Title: Inside China's Forbidden City.

DS795.8.F67M37 2008
951'.03—dc22
2007022413

Book design by Maria T. Middleton

Printed and bound in China
10 9 8 7 6 5 4 3 2 1

harry n. abrams, inc.
a subsidiary of La Martinière Groupe
115 West 18th Street
New York, NY 10011
www.hnabooks.com